P9-CQH-206

...p... io ... vogli essere de...si...

...no mini ... sta molto loquente di salvar...

...la quantità de danari ... io voleuo ... no au...

...ssi al bancho ... io ui dicho ... e danari della p...

al papa io gli piglierò p poterlo seruire meglio

... e p potere tornare nella chasa

...giouanni detto e se papa le dette principio

...e dia io a mi chontento di quelgi ... sua

...e p ... io credo ... e fatci bene ... e ...

...inciare altrimenti ne prima ne poi e lo

... io nebbi ... ora otto mesi guardate

...uostre e se auete chomessione dateme

...uien ... io ... ma non tocha insino aggi se no tan...

...mente arrossi ... me basta ... e no si ...

...habbi ... e chosi me forza ...

...ma questi fichatione

...cho più della lettera ... io mi ... lagnio ...

...di romani a dì 18 d'ottobre 152... ...

...saluati lapportatore ...

J. Patrick Lewis

Michelangelo's World

CREATIVE EDITIONS

For Rita Marshall and Aaron Frisch, without whom... J.P.L.

Text copyright © 2007 J. Patrick Lewis

Published in 2007 by Creative Editions

P.O. Box 227, Mankato, MN 56002 USA

Creative Editions is an imprint of The Creative Company.

Designed by Rita Marshall, Edited by Aaron Frisch

Photographs by Alamy Images (Arco Images, Classic Images, Mary Evans Picture Library, Scala, Visual Arts Library),

Bridgeman Art Library (p. 1 Study of Warrior's Head, Buonarroti, Michelangelo (1475-1564) / British Museum,

London, UK; p. 2 1895-9-15-503 W.34v Page of handwriting, Buonarroti, Michelangelo (1475-1564) /

British museum, London, UK; p. 3 Hands of God and Adam, detail from The Creation of Adam,

from the Sistine Ceiling, 1511 (fresco) (post-restoration), Buonarroti, Michelangelo (1475-1564) /

Vatican Museums and Galleries, Vatican City, Italy; p. 6 Head of the 'Manhattan' Cupid, c. 1494-96

(marble) (detail), Buonarroti, Michelangelo (1475-1564) (attr.to) / Louvre, Paris, France;

p. 14 Portrait Study of a Young Boy, c. 1532 (black chalk on paper), Buonarroti, Michelangelo (1475-1564) /

British Museum, London, UK; p. 21 David, detail of the head of Michelangelo Buonarroti (1475-1564),

1504 (marble), Buonarroti, Michelangelo (1475-1564) / Galleria dell' Accademia, Florence, Italy; p. 24-25

Sistine Chapel ceiling and lunettes, 1508-12 (fresco) (post-restoration), Buonarroti, Michelangelo (1475-1564) /

Vatican Museums and Galleries, Vatican City, Italy; p. 26 Head of Satyr (pen & ink on paper) (b/w photo),

Buonarroti, Michelangelo (1475-1564) / Louvre, Paris, France, Giraudon; p. 27 Ideal Head, c. 1518-20

(red chalk on paper), Buonarroti, Michelangelo (1475-1564) / Ashmolean Museum, University of Oxford, UK;

p. 28 Sistine Chapel Ceiling: Delphic Sibyl (fresco), Buonarroti, Michelangelo (1475-1564) /

Vatican Museum and Galleries, Vatican City, Italy, Alinari; p. 30 Tomb of Pope Julius II (1453-1513)

detail of the head of Moses, 1513-16 (marble), Buonarroti, Michelangelo (1475-1564) / San Pietro in Vincoli,

Rome, Italy, Alinari; p. 31 Tomb of Pope Julius II (1453-1513) detail of Moses, 1513-16

(marble), Buonarroti, Michelangelo (1475-1564) / San Pietro in Vincoli, Rome, Italy, Alinari), Corbis

(Archivo Iconografico, Bettmann, Vittoriano Rastelli, Ted Spiegel, Gustavo Tomsich, World Films Enterprises)

Illustrations © 2007 Etienne Delessert (Cover, p. 38-39), © 2007 Gary Kelley (p. 9)

All rights reserved. No part of the contents of this book may be reproduced by any means

without the written permission of the publisher. Printed in Italy

Library of Congress Cataloging-in-Publication Data

Lewis, J. Patrick. Michelangelo's world / by J. Patrick Lewis. Includes bibliographical references.

ISBN-13: 978-1-56846-167-0

1. Michelangelo Buonarroti, 1475-1564—Juvenile literature.

2. Artists—Italy—Biography—Juvenile literature.

I. Michelangelo Buonarroti, 1475-1564. II. Title.

N6923.B9L48 2007   700.92—dc22 [B]   2006027666

First edition 9 8 7 6 5 4 3 2 1

Table of Contents

Head of Cupid

Introduction

"I saw the angel in the marble and carved until I set him free."

Michelangelo

Among the world's artistic geniuses, Michelangelo di Lodovico Buonarroti (1475–1564) was possibly the greatest of them all. Unlike his contemporaries and those who came after him, he excelled in sculpture, painting, and architecture, not to mention poetry—a versatility that made him a true Renaissance man.

What is most notable in his art is what has kept him fresh and astonishing half a millennium after his death: the marriage of physical beauty and spiritual revelation. But there is also the conflict of good and evil, love and hate, exaltation and despair, all of which seemed to mirror his own anxieties.

He capped his long career with that stunning symbol of Renaissance art, the dome of St. Peter's Basilica in Rome, but there were so many riches that preceded it. The entire art world held its breath in the face of such virtuosity. It was as if art had reinvented itself with Michelangelo as its spark. He wrote hundreds of marvelous poems and sonnets, too, adding an exclamation point to an output of artwork that many—both during his lifetime and since—believed was perfection itself.

What follows is a small homage in sonnets to Michelangelo's world.

J.P.L.

Michelangelo's Birth
March 6, 1475

There in the village of Caprese, a part

Of remote Tuscany, the mountains wild

Revealed the gift—a Universal Child,

Whose name is now synonymous with art.

In that same year, oh, other things occurred.

Old wars resumed, new battles won and lost,

Far distant lands explored and rivers crossed.

But only he became a household word.

What is it that explains the truly great?

The finest arts endure, they never die.

Pure genius suddenly appears, but why?

Perhaps it's that the future cannot wait.

The Buonarroti family could not know

The son to come had centuries to go.

Born about fifty miles southeast of Florence, Michelangelo was the second of five children. He was nursed by the daughter of a stonecutter, perhaps because of his mother's poor health. The family soon moved to Florence, where they lived in genteel poverty. He enjoyed a close boyhood friendship with Francesco Granacci (1469–1543), a graceful young painter, who recognized Michelangelo's genius and introduced him to the excellent artist Domenico Ghirlandaio (1449–1494).

PISA

ARNO RIVER

FIRENZE (FLORENCE)

BIBBONA

BOLGHERI

SAN GIMIGNANO

CASTAGNETO CARDUCCI

CHIANTI

CAPRESE

SIENA

ELBA

TOSCANA

ROMA (ROME)

N

Years of Youth
1485–1495

Against his father's wishes, Michelangelo entered
Ghirlandaio's workshop in 1487, apprenticed for three
years, and learned the art of panel painting and fresco.
Later, the powerful Medici family, which was led by
Lorenzo de' Medici (1449–1492), invited him to live
at the family palace. Still in his teens, Michelangelo
completed the *Madonna of the Stairs* and the *Battle of
the Centaurs*, which firmly established his prowess as
a sculptor.

If I am good for anything, he said,

It is because of such fine mountain air...

And being suckled in stonecutters' care,

The hammers sweetly ringing in my head.

I climbed the years and scaled the favored hill,

Inquisitive of every quarried stone.

Apprenticed young, I came into my own

In Ghirlandaio's studio until

Lorenzo the Magnificent, who ruled

Florence, one of the glowing Medici,

Would offer me his home, where I was schooled

And dusted with ambition properly.

The lesson I learned there was simply this:

A sculptor's world is work. And work is bliss.

Of the many intricate details on the Sistine Chapel's ceiling, there is

one above all that lives on in posterity—*The Creation of Adam*.

Here, God, floating through the heavens, reaches down to touch

Adam's fingertips as the mortal reclines on the empty coast of earth.

Michelangelo's deep religious conviction is on display here with per-

haps greater force and purity than in anything else he ever produced.

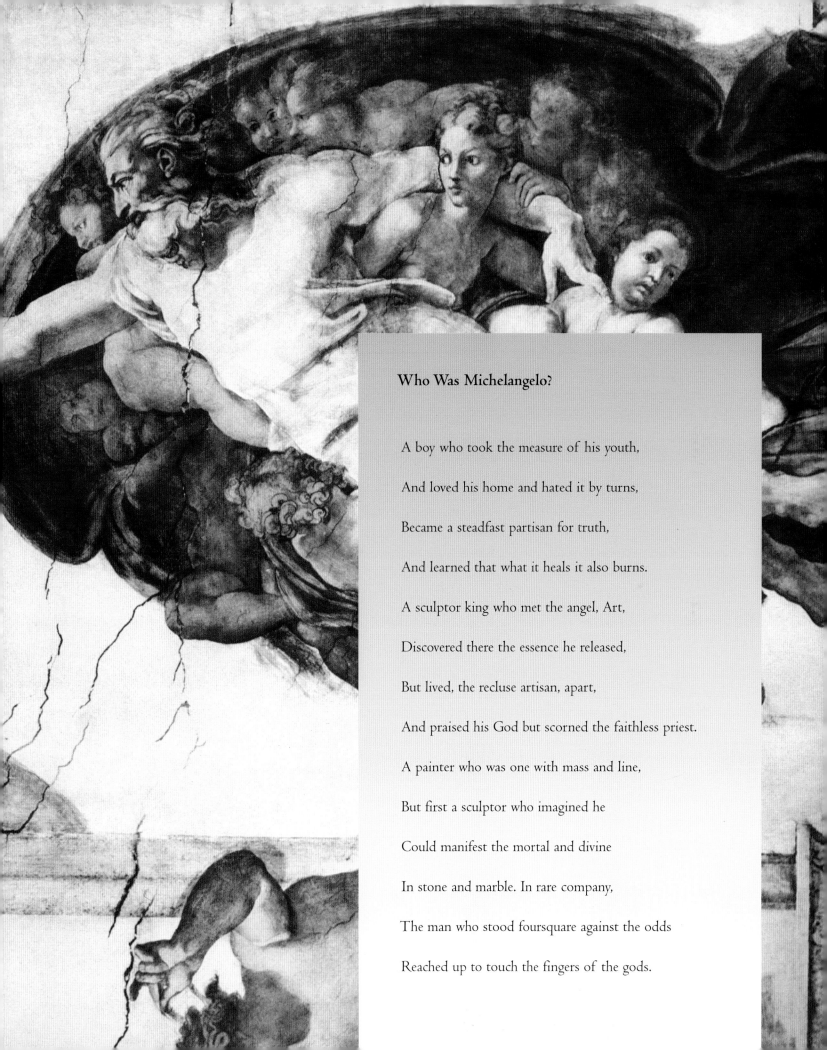

Who Was Michelangelo?

A boy who took the measure of his youth,

And loved his home and hated it by turns,

Became a steadfast partisan for truth,

And learned that what it heals it also burns.

A sculptor king who met the angel, Art,

Discovered there the essence he released,

But lived, the recluse artisan, apart,

And praised his God but scorned the faithless priest.

A painter who was one with mass and line,

But first a sculptor who imagined he

Could manifest the mortal and divine

In stone and marble. In rare company,

The man who stood foursquare against the odds

Reached up to touch the fingers of the gods.

Alternately described as short-tempered, arrogant, and aloof, Michelangelo did not suffer incompetence gladly. He demanded excellence of every artist, especially himself, and his perfectionism could rile others; a fellow student in the Medici gardens, Pietro Torrigiano (1472–1522), three years his senior, once punched Michelangelo so hard that the blow broke his nose, which remained permanently crooked.

Study of a young boy

14

On Friendship

His mother died when he was only six.

His father, stern and cold, expecting much

Of him, did not possess a father's touch.

Fill in the blank with what such life predicts.

Later, when it was said the artist could

Be temperamental, difficult and rude,

Reflecting badly on an attitude

As unforgiving as his childhood,

He vowed that "more than any man alive

I care deeply for every human being."

Beyond his art and architecture, warm,

Abiding friendships could barely survive,

Ironically for him who savored seeing

The beautiful and true in human form.

The *Pietá*
Marble, Rome, 1498–1500

A youth so incorruptible and pure

That she could be "the daughter of her Son"

Has conquered grief. Cut and polished to one

Indomitable spirit to endure,

Emmarbled softly in her drapery,

The Virgin Mary most demurely flaunts

Visions of Dante and the High Renaissance:

Beauty, restraint and classic harmony.

Like breath distilled from stone, perfectly framed

By Michelangelo in sculptured space,

Christ seems to seek his mother's sure embrace,

Alive five Roman centuries in famed

St. Peter's. There enchanted pilgrims find

The only work of art he ever signed.

In 1497, a French cardinal offered Michelangelo a commission to sculpt the Virgin Mary with the dead Christ. So Michelangelo went to a town called Carrara in a valley of the Apennines that was well known for its brittle, hard-to-work white marble. What he created demonstrates his unparalleled understanding of human anatomy. Later, he carved his name in Latin on the sash running diagonally across the Virgin's bosom.

In 1501, Michelangelo returned to Florence, homesick for the city of his youth. He acquired a piece of white marble 18 feet high and weighing several tons, and set to work carving David on September 13, 1501. As Leonardo da Vinci's (1452–1519) *Last Supper*, *Mona Lisa*, and other great works of art were a part of this period, the date marks the beginning of the High Renaissance. The *David*'s strapping manhood radiates enormous will and awesome power—what the Italians call *terribilita*—a characteristic Michelangelo himself, though he was only 5-foot-4, was often said to possess.

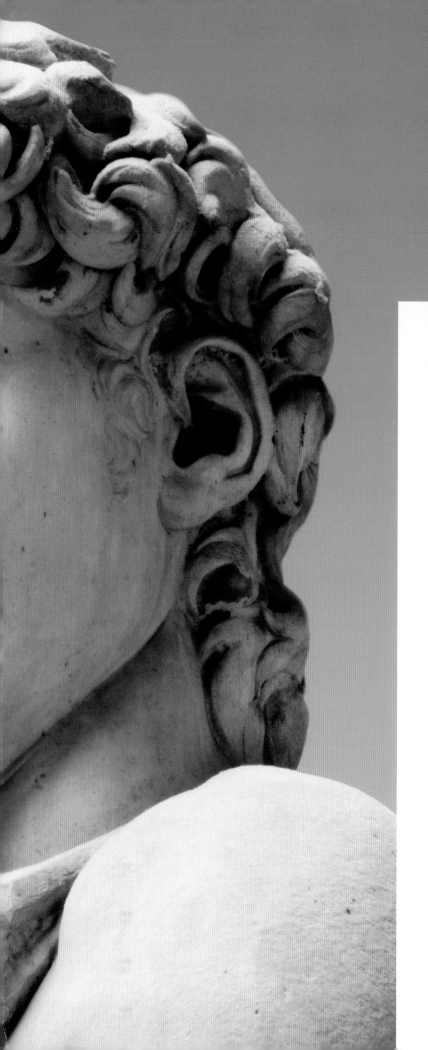

The *David*
Marble, Florence, 1501–1504

Great Florence of 500 years ago,

A city-state exposed to mortal threat

And facing bleak uncertainty, was yet

Possessed of courage. Michelangelo

At once fastened idea to ideal—

Fortezza (strength) molded to cleverness.

His larger than life *David* would impress

Eternity, a masterful appeal

To readiness *before* a war was fought—

Not afterwards, when, apprehension fled,

Our vanity surveys the severed head.

Gazing on the boy-giant comes this thought:

The distant past is never far away—

Tomorrow is foretold in yesterday.

Painted to celebrate the marriage of prosperous weaver Agnolo Doni and Maddalena Strozzi, the *Doni Tondo*, sometimes called the *Doni Madonna*, stresses a key aspect of Michelangelo's work. The nude figures confirm his belief that the human body is the temple of the soul. In this, his first great painting, the five naked youths, like Greek heroes, could be angels, men preparing for baptism, or merely a demonstration of man's inherent nobility.

The *Doni Tondo*
Tempera on Panel, c. 1504

When Leonardo painted long ago

The *Mona Lisa*, Michelangelo

Was conscious of his rival genius who

Made miracles of everything he drew.

The *Doni Tondo* (*tondo* meaning "round")—

His only finished painting to be found

On neither wall nor ceiling—may not be

The best example of his legacy.

Still, later painters seeking to depict

The Holy Family felt it—something clicked.

The mind's eye blinked. Old Masters so inclined

To draw *Madonnas* easily divined

From memory this marvelous tableau

Indubitably Michelangelo.

Head of a Satyr

Ideal head

This sonnet describes but a few of the obstacles facing Michelangelo beneath the Sistine ceiling: the weather, lack of money, standing and looking upward on scaffolding sixty feet in the air (all day, as he said of himself, "My beard points to heaven…."), the toll it took on one's body and mind, and the unending loneliness. At the midway point, the pope visited him, impatiently wondering when he would finish. "When I can!" Michelangelo replied angrily, to which the pope responded by striking him with his cane.

Painting on High
Vatican, Rome, 1508–1512

The obstacles before him grew ten-fold.

His five assistants soon proved a disgrace.

In winter the Sistine was bitter cold—

A hundred braziers could not warm the place.

He stood up, painting, high above the floor

And suffered vertigo. The pigments dripped

And spattered on his face a rich decor.

Lacking money, which left him ill-equipped,

He begged the Pope unceasingly for more.

Broken in body and spirit, he withstood

Temptation to resign the awesome chore,

Still doubting whether it was any good.

And yet he meant to break the ceiling's spell

"Lonely as a hangman," said Raphael.

The Fall of Man

Some suggest that the *Moses* is Michelangelo's greatest sculpture. The perfect detail of the Old Testament prophet, twice human scale, relaxing with his fingers stroking his beard, is genius in stone. The horns protruding from his head are a mistake of the Latin Vulgate Bible. "Rays of light" in Hebrew was erroneously translated in the Vulgate as "horns."

Moses
Marble, Rome, c. 1513–1516

The experts all agree on his great art,

The *Pietá*, the *David*, the Sistine,

And, twice as large as life to swell the scene,

Colossal *Moses*, fiery counterpart

Of Pope and sculptor both—a work of heart

One hundred inches high. Sitting between

Two lesser mortals, Moses might have been

For Michelangelo merely the start

Of his ambitious plan to celebrate

The life and death of Julius the Second with

A massive forty-figure tomb. But time

And politics conspired to alter fate.

The master leaped beyond the rim of myth:

The commonplace for him became sublime.

Vittoria Colonna

On Love

If Michelangelo desired a Muse,

Vittoria Colonna was her name.

He and the Roman lady found their views

On literature, love, life and death the same.

Though castles, palaces and wealth were hers,

She lived a quiet, cloistered life and wrote

Religious poetry. Biographers

Have said Vittoria was his grace note.

And then he met his masculine ideal,

A schoolboy, Tommaso dei Cavalieri.

But iron will and courage would conceal

His passion. Isn't it extraordinary

So late in one's focused life to think twice

Of love worthy of earth and paradise?

Vittoria Colonna

We can learn a great deal about Michelangelo's work and life from his poems and letters. On the subject of marriage, he once said: "I already have a wife who is too much for me; she is my art, and my works are my children." His two dearest friends and confidantes were Vittoria Colonna (1492–1547), noblewoman and poet, and the devoted Tommaso dei Cavalieri (1509–1587), 34 years younger than Michelangelo, who kept a bedside vigil at the painter's death.

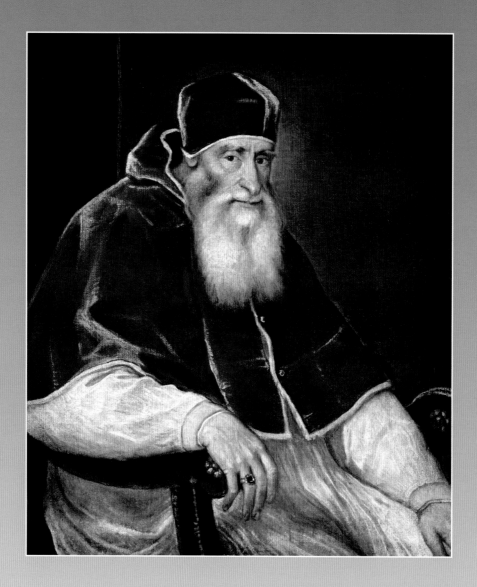

Last Judgment
Vatican, Rome, 1536–1541

Pope Paul the Third strongly expressed a hope:

Immortalize my papal legacy,

Dear Michelangelo, kaleidoscope

Redemption, heaven, hell—eternity.

A theme of such significance might look

Like Brueghel, Bosch, or else, perhaps a Blake.

With his *Last Judgment*, though, he wrote the book—

A visionary's Scripture, for God's sake.

Morality police were scandalized.

They covered up the nakedness years hence.

What is the meaning of Christ "sanitized"?

The triumph of the censor over sense.

But oh the awful glory that remains—

The sacred sky through art's great windowpanes.

In 1534, Pope Paul III (1468–1549) asked

Michelangelo to paint the altar wall of the Sistine

Chapel—more than 2,000 square feet. The task took

him longer to complete than the entire ceiling itself.

Upon seeing the fresco, the pope reacted to its gloom

and terror by falling on his knees in awe. For there, look-

ing down, was an all-powerful Christ, and every figure

was in motion—the risen, the sinners, and the angels.

The Last Judgment

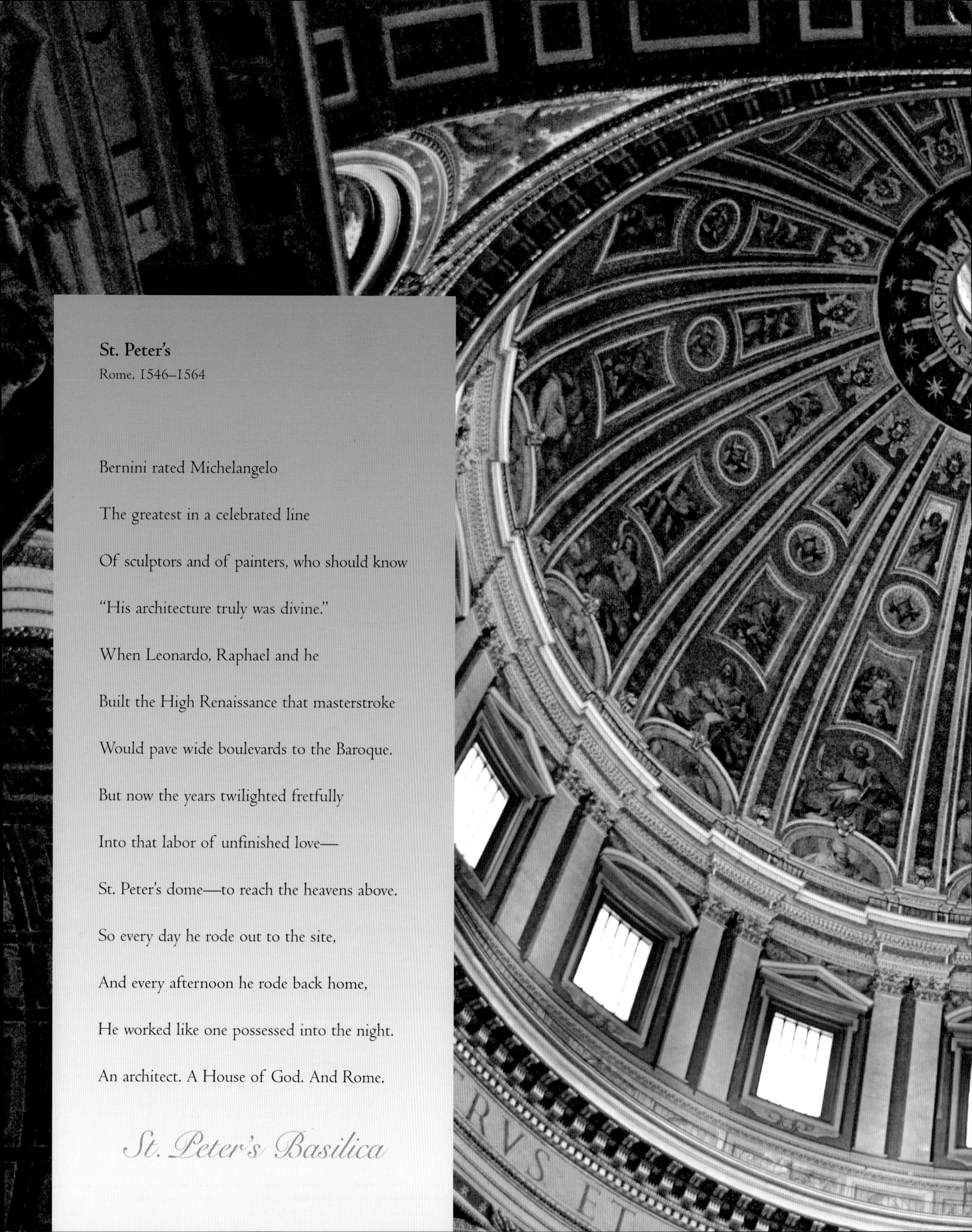

St. Peter's
Rome, 1546–1564

Bernini rated Michelangelo

The greatest in a celebrated line

Of sculptors and of painters, who should know

"His architecture truly was divine."

When Leonardo, Raphael and he

Built the High Renaissance that masterstroke

Would pave wide boulevards to the Baroque.

But now the years twilighted fretfully

Into that labor of unfinished love—

St. Peter's dome—to reach the heavens above.

So every day he rode out to the site,

And every afternoon he rode back home,

He worked like one possessed into the night.

An architect. A House of God. And Rome.

St. Peter's Basilica

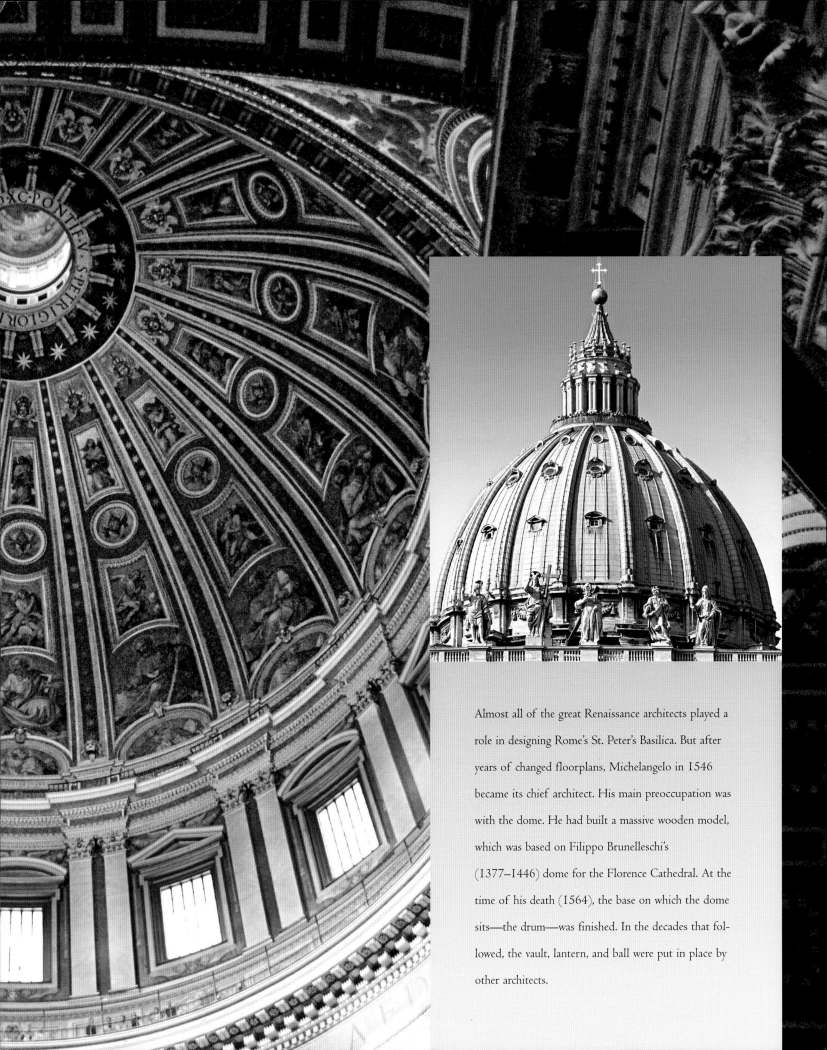

Almost all of the great Renaissance architects played a role in designing Rome's St. Peter's Basilica. But after years of changed floorplans, Michelangelo in 1546 became its chief architect. His main preoccupation was with the dome. He had built a massive wooden model, which was based on Filippo Brunelleschi's (1377–1446) dome for the Florence Cathedral. At the time of his death (1564), the base on which the dome sits—the drum—was finished. In the decades that followed, the vault, lantern, and ball were put in place by other architects.

Michelangelo's Death
February 18, 1564

A week before he died, chiseling yet

Another *Pietá*, he soon fell ill,

Ingested herbs, seawater and hope until

His figure turned a pale silhouette.

He had two sets of poems and drawings burned

Against the wishes of his patrons, and

Regretted dying just before he'd learned

"The alphabet of my profession." Planned

His will: three sentences. He left his soul

To God, his body to the earth, the rest

Of his possessions to his kin. The whole

Of humankind was not left dispossessed:

He gave to time what few of us can give,

The man who died had centuries to live.

Michelangelo

During his last years, Michelangelo carved three more *Pietás* while supervising work on St. Peter's. He died at the age of 88, surrounded by his family and a few close friends, and was buried in the Church of Santa Croce in Florence.

Bibliography

Beck, James, *Three Worlds of Michelangelo*, Norton, 1999.

Bull, George, *Michelangelo: A Biography*, St. Martin's Press, 1995.

Coughlan, Robert, et al., *The World of Michelangelo: 1475–1564*, Time-Life Books, 1966.

Di Cagno, Gabriella, *Masters of Art: Michelangelo*, Peter Bedrick Books, 1996.

Hartt, Frederick, *Michelangelo Buonarroti*, Abrams, 2004.

Hibbard, Howard, *Michelangelo*, Harper & Row, 1974.

McLanathan, Richard, *Michelangelo: First Impressions*, Abrams, 1993.

Nims, John Frederick (tr.), *The Complete Poems of Michelangelo*, University of Chicago Press, 1998.

Stanley, Diane, *Michelangelo*, HarperCollins, 2000.

Stone, Irving, *The Agony and the Ecstasy*, Doubleday and Company, 1961.